Or/And POEMS
Jeannine Marie Pitas

IRON
PEN

PARACLETE PRESS
BREWSTER, MASSACHUSETTS

To Elfie S. Raymond
(1931–2012),
in memoriam

———

Para Magdalena Cuyuch Corío, tu familia y tu futuro,
con todo mi amor, respeto y gratitud.

2023 First Printing

Or/And: Poems

Copyright © 2023 by Jeannine M. Pitas

ISBN 978-1-64060-790-3

The Iron Pen name and logo are trademarks of Paraclete Press.

Library of Congress LCCN 2022045279

10 9 8 7 6 5 4 3 2 1

Published by Paraclete Press
Brewster, Massachusetts
www.paracletepress.com

CONTENTS

1 Madonna
of the Two Scars

2
Combustion

3
I Do

1
Madonna of the
Two Scars

Wings of Desire

An angel whispers to readers in the library.
He's tired of everyone wanting something different.

A trapeze artist dressed like an angel
doesn't know that real angels are wingless.

I wait for my photo at the machine
and emerge with another face.

This is the world of one-shoed walkers
who shade themselves with borrowed umbrellas,

sign their names with dropped pens,
open doors with lost keys.

Stones come alive. Time can't heal.
No, time's the illness.

The first strands of gray hair. An old photo album.
The lost storyteller, lost peace.

A blue ocean, sky. Afternoon coffees.
Cuban cigars. Dragons. A bed.

The world that shrinks to the size of a room.
The choir of young women who come to sing.

The grass tall enough to hide
or make love in.

The deep, fast river you crossed easily
because your beloved was waiting on the other side.

An immortal singer turned organ grinder,
ignored or mocked.

Abandoned railroad tracks. The other side.
The crucifix hanging from the classroom wall.

The plaid uniform your grandmother starched.
Borders. A country with as many states

as there are citizens. Rags pledged to each morning,
folded each afternoon. Shibboleths.

Barbed wire. Private security guards.
The world in color. Sunsets, lonely rooms.

Cherry cough drops. A nurse's kind face.
Your final bed. The lamp turned off.

June 24

Feast of St. John the Baptist

Today my head has been removed,
traded for a jug of wine, a pluck
of the lyre, a young girl's careless
dance. In Orthodox icons I hold
myself on a platter; faithful ones
bend forward to kiss. I never knew
this was the price of living
on locusts and wild honey, for preparing
my cousin the carpenter's way. Today the light
begins its slow death; I know
I will rise again. In two thousand years, a girl
who bears my name will dance
around a bonfire, surrounded by old men and women,
tiniest children, dancers on stilts, young
girls in white dresses with ivy crowns.
She will whirl and whirl, dizzyingly dance
and dance, exalting in her own beauty.
The price will be her head.

A man she thought she loved
will smash her into a wall
and her head will fall off.
She will pick it up, carry it in
a backpack or purse while a replacement
is fitted over the space. Years later, again
on my day, she will sit on a bench on Aliki Peninsula
beside the marble ruins of a basilica
made in my cousin's name.

She will look at the columns and archways, watch
summer's highest, brightest light fall
on olive trees. I will come to her,
take her hand. When I wipe away
the painted face, she will open
her purse and offer me
the torn head she holds. My cousin
will come to help me. We will lift it,
place it on her shoulders, suture that wound
as all the scarved women
lighting candles before Orthodox icons
have done for me. We will help her
to her feet, beckon her to join us
in our search for others
who've lost their heads.

Once you have seen the beatific vision...

It's hard to go back. If among ancient red rocks, between sun and moon, you've felt the forces that run through the skin of lizards and cacti as well as your own, it's no fun returning to opaque city smog. If you've looked up at stars and remembered to thank the light that lets us move, it's not easy to move again among the thankless. If you have felt the warmth from lava under your feet, it's hard to believe in the pairs we form. Plato's *Symposium* did not quite get it. We are not severed eight-limbed creatures; we are broken million-pointed stars. We yearn for our original light.

Panic

I met Pan when I was 21. It's said he, god of shepherds, can be found in mountain fields, but I encountered him on my college campus, in a hidden quad behind a stone building with icicles dangling from the roof, tiny daggers. It was winter. He came alone. He struck me with his staff and gave me altitude; my insides crumpled like autumn's last falling leaf, shriveled as a sheet of ice hit my shoulder. I lay there. The snow shone gold; the treetops blazed, but no voice emerged from within them, no all-important "I am." Just the opposite: "I am not." This is not me. I shook and saw a strange aura around myself, a halo of gold and green. Rats and mice nipped my toes; the ground opened to reveal sharp rocks waiting to tear me into sinews and blood. Beneath them a blue sea waited to caress me and not let go, beauty and terror both too close. At last he turned away. It took a few minutes to trust he wouldn't be back. The mountain flattened; the blazing trees regained their green. In the distance I heard the bells of sheep, their gentle bleating. A blue sky entered my insides. I stood; I could feel the halo still around me. I could still smell the aroma of meadows after winter's melting, of soft trilliums drinking the sun between the branches of skeletal trees; I could taste the first mint leaves. Lush pastures rolled through my stomach; my heart broke into cumulus clouds; pink mimosa flowers sprung from my hands. My lungs were filled with the blueness of early spring.

Ghost Dance Krakowiak

Ribboned braids. No fancy dance. Mazurka spun on wobbling knees. 1873: my great-great-uncle, a Polish priest, founded St. Stanislaus Church in Buffalo, NY. Born here, raised here: I used to say my ancestors were back in Poland during the crime. But Poland wasn't a country then. From colonized land, to colonized land: my priest-uncle landed in a genocide. They say he went to greet Polish immigrants at Buffalo's train station, brought them to the city, their new settlement. His English was good. 1890: what did he think, reading headlines about Wounded Knee? Did he turn away, "It's not my concern?" Did he mutter, in Polish, "Serves those heathens right?" Did he feel any pang, any sense that his Jesus might not approve? He has made it into some history books, but this story isn't there. My Babcia might have known it, but she died a century after that crime. I suspect he believed "this land is my land," though he never heard the Guthrie song. My mother grew up singing it, and "O Columbia the Gem of the Ocean," while still learning her parents' native tongue. She passed that knotted language on to me, along with those slippery songs. My great-uncle was of no one place. Despite what my passport says, neither am I. The beaded vest I wore as a child, the lacy apron that flew as I whirled in the traditional Polish dances: Krakowiak, Kujawiak, Mazurka, Polonez—behind them moved another dance, one that did not belong to me. I could feel it deep in my skin, my bones: the Ghost Dance of those who prayed to be saved, who begged with their bodies for my people—*my* people—to leave them alone at last. It haunts each dance I do, the polka and waltz of my youth, the salsa and tango and blues I learn today. Red ribbons spin like blood. Ghosts continue to dance. They twist through each step and won't go away.

Nephophobia

Fear of Clouds

I need to move to Arizona
but can't afford it.
Buffalo, New York, is where I'm stuck.

Buffalo, land of misty
lake effects, seven days
without the sun.

Day and night, day
and night, they cast their shadows
over the land. I fear those too.

People would laugh if they knew
this is why I can't hold down
a job, why the computer's glare

is my refuge, why I stare at the
goldfish bowl and watch the white-and-
orange striped creatures open

and close their mouths. They're not stupid.
They must know they're getting nowhere
as they circle around that bowl.

I can't recall how it first started –
maybe my first airplane flight
when we spent what felt like hours

inside, when I learned they weren't
made from cotton candy, that if the plane's engine
were turned off, we would fall.

Maybe it was when I learned that rain
wasn't sent by Jesus sprinkling us
with some heavenly baptism.

Maybe it was the time when, while walking
the dog, I got caught in the rain
and saw lightning electrocute the ground.

Cumulus, soft, fake comfort; nimbus, thick
with anger, stratus, cold foreboding.
Cirrus are the worst, wispy fingers

of some divine monster
I may or may not meet.
I ask for the purity of open blue,

clarity, light. I ask for the security
of a rainless sky. And yet there's much
I miss—green reeds under fresh water

I'd wade in, jeweled sand, soft algae
and ferns that caress my feet,
the smell of mint and

lavender, everything I can't
bring in. I miss
the moon.

Mycophobia

Fear of Mushrooms
For Margaret Randall

They are made of death.

I knew that
before anyone told me.

They do not belong
in the lush green of the forest,

among these ferns,
these conifers, this smell

of maple leaves and holly. They surge
in the night, surrounding me

with a constant fear
of what I will become.

For years I didn't understand
my fear, until the day I learned

the truth: before I could speak,
one entrusted to love me

held me down, placed a terrible
mushroom deep in my mouth, and choked

my narrow throat. It was too much reality
for a three-year-old in a pink party dress,

patent leather shoes, too soon for one
so recently born to be thrust

into death's slippery truth.
Language was what let me out;

words were the breadcrumbs
I followed to escape

the cannibal witch's cottage,
the wizard's laboratory of poisons.

But even today the path is still lined
with those horrid white weapons,

those terrible stalks
that sprout up

from the dead.

What Rafa Writes

Managua, Nicaragua, July 2018

"My country is burning."

I sift through pictures
of singed cars,
protesters running from riot police,
shredded flags.

Ten years ago
I came to your country
to teach English to the rich
and plant the occasional mango tree.

I climbed your volcanoes, marched
through the streets to the cathedral
in the Good Friday procession,
admired your blue-green national bird.

So many mornings
I lay in a hammock in the garden
and said the whole world
should be this way.

I knew nothing then
of William Walker, Somoza,
Iran-Contra, The School of the Americas,
The Central American Free Trade Agreement.

We met one Saturday morning
at the Centro para Niños Abandonados
where I taught English
even though you were not at all abandonado.

You had two sisters and a mother
who worked sixteen-hour days sewing at the maquila
while you dreamed of crossing borders
and earning the money to let her stay home.

I promised to help you
but then went back
to skyscrapers and Sephora,
Nordstrom and Starbucks,

to a university library
shaped like a peacock
where I hid
behind novels and poems.

Today you write, "Two hundred sixty-four
have died. Hundreds more
have disappeared. Priests and nuns fear
for their lives. You wouldn't recognize this place."

Today you're twenty-four,
the age I was
when I first taught you
the English alphabet.

I picture the bus you're boarding
mustard-yellow
discarded from a school district
in Kansas or Delaware.

You tell me you're seeking a new life
in Panama or Costa Rica.
My country—the one you dreamed of—
refuses to let you in.

Garlic

Cancer fighter. Memory booster. Vampire defeater. Base of the fettucine alfredo, lasagna, gallo pinto. *You can never have too much garlic*, my mother assured me every time I put one extra clove into the sauce. But when Magdalena moves in, she tells me "no." *I like the taste, just not the smell.* At first I don't understand. Garlic-breath never bothers me; I never worry about an offensive kiss. Magdalena, maker of tamales with mushrooms, chicken soup punctured by the hottest chilies shipped by her mother in Guatemala—the reddest reds, the spiciest pimiento—waits a year before telling me the reason. *When we were crossing the border, we stuffed our pockets and shoes with garlic. It was meant to keep the dogs away.* My smile vanishes; jokes about vampires shrivel and fade like the bodies of the dead as my favorite food turns to pungent white pain. Today Magdalena no longer shares my home; the smell of her chili no longer waters my eyes. She has moved to another house, in hiding from the ones who would seize and jail her. Garlic again fills my soups and stews, but the delight is tinged with yearning for a world without desert walls, without dogs bred cruel, a world where imaginary lines don't stop anyone from breathing.

During the Sixth Extinction

For Mary Colwell

A woman walks a thousand miles
along the coasts of England and Ireland
telling people about curlews.

We have seven years left
to save them. "These birds mean
something to us," she says.

I think of her journey
as I watch the milkweed
lie in wait for the occasional monarch.

I'm not sure when it changed.
I'm not sure when dark summer nights
were bereft of fireflies, when

monarchs' black and orange faces
started appearing
on missing person posters.

I don't know when bats' swooping
dives diminished, when they stopped writing
calligraphy on their night flights,

I don't know when the clover receded,
when frogs began to disappear,
when the great herds of caribou diminished by half.

I do know when Mary Oliver died,
that precious poet so many roll their eyes at,
her grace too easily graspable

to seem true.
What was the last thing she saw
when there were no more chevrons

gliding over the lake,
when there weren't
enough flapping wings

for any of us to find
in the passage of their flight
our names?

Garbage Envy

I open a door and find a wall behind it.

I try to meditate when walking, to thank the ground for each step. But that doesn't stop me from tripping on a loose stone. The sidewalk and the sky turn sideways as I fall.

I'm caught in a knot. It's made of my own choices. Each tiny decision—which street to walk down, when to set my alarm—is another thread that wraps itself around me, entwines me, covers my eyes. Mary, Untier of Knots, pray for me. Will she? Perhaps.

The knot unravels and all of a sudden there is snow on the ground. A robotic garbage truck is picking up the week's waste. Where will it go? I picture it driving and driving, farther south, flying on metallic wings through an imaginary net that would trap me if I followed. It drives to a place without snow, down to a plaza filled with drums and dancers, a plaza in a place I once called home.

The garbage truck crosses those imaginary lines, dumps that garbage right in the square. This is how it has been for five hundred years at least, garbage from the snowy places getting dumped on the lands of sun. They think they can send trash away, but it stays even if we won't see it.

I never thought I'd envy garbage. A plastic bag can fly where it wants. I can't.

Letters

My mother complains she can't read my handwriting.
She says it's a scrawl like a doctor's. When I point out

that I am a doctor, she rolls her eyes. Apparently a Ph.D.
doesn't count. She was taught the right way. In the 1950s.

By nuns. I say I can't read hers either, and it's less beautiful
than she thinks. "It's still better than yours," she retorts.

Alas, I can't disagree. As for my father, he barely writes at all—
he only lifts a pen to pay a bill, sign his name.

The students I teach send text messages in class.
They complain if I make them hand-write a test. They barely

learned cursive in school. Sometimes I feel like one of the last
monks still decorating manuscripts, long after Gutenberg's

disruption. I know this is an old person's sentiment.
I prefer to type my prose, but I always hand-write poems.

My numbers look like half-open windows, flags
of countries that don't exist anymore. My letters

look like hitchhikers standing at the side of the road,
or old friends waving goodbye, smaller and smaller

as the car pulls away.

River Rooms

She's standing in the kitchen with her friend. They're about to make curried potatoes, and she's ashamed to admit she doesn't know how to cook. Her mother wanted her to learn, but she resisted, just as she resisted shaving legs or plucking eyebrows or anything that would make her too conventionally feminine. She's paying for it now, twenty-two and clueless. Her room is a box, a box within a box; she's happy as hell to be in a box, doing something with her life, conjugating her grandmother's verbs by day and learning to cook by night. There's no refrigerator in these rooms, so she leaves her food on the seventh-floor balcony and hopes for the best. Sometimes, when washing her clothes, she likes to stand on that same balcony and wring each separate garment, watching the droplets as they splatter to the ground below. She enjoys these moments of subtlety. She likes to stare out at her life ahead.

The river I fly over
is the Wisła
everything's a blanket
everything's a box
full of dragons—
the same dragon that once flamed
over Wawel hill
now safely stowed away
alongside the fireplace.
I fly over you
back past the castles, the churches
back past the university that Queen Jadwiga
relinquished her jewels for
back past all the yellow boxes

cluttering communist weeds
sprung up where enchanted forests
once grew.

The room is white. She's sitting with Sam at the kitchen table. Cristina
left early—her job starts at 7 a.m. Both of them—Cristina and Sam—
are mad at her for not doing her share of the chores, but lately she's been
better at it. She and Sam are eating toast with butter when it comes. A
knock. Once, twice. Their eyes meet. Don't open it, his glance affirms.
They've been warned. They live in a transitional neighborhood. Any
guest they knew would call ahead. She is not dissuaded; she has to see,
to know. She stands, peeks through the peephole. There's a robber on
the other side. In his hand he holds a knife. He doesn't see her looking.
He knocks again. She goes back to the table, sits. Her eyes lock with
Sam's. They wait. They wait. Minutes, hours, years have gone by; she
and Sam don't even speak anymore, but still she sits there waiting. The
knocking hasn't stopped.

The river I fly over
is Río Uruguay.
Salto, I am coming for you
even though you no longer
wait for me.
the Southern Cross
has settled, and people don't need
a town where time has stopped.
Among the conifers and
palms I landed, along that river
of painted birds—
how I yearned
to be one of them.

She wanted a home with you. All of them did, but it's not possible to speak about the others. She did. She wouldn't give you a key. She wouldn't let you move in your things. She was ashamed of herself as well as you, of her desire, of the fire that shivered beneath this valley's heat. She was ashamed that rosaries weren't enough for her, Bibles weren't enough for her, students and work and a big fat paycheck and Esperanza's delectable nacatamales weren't enough. She needed bachata, she needed machetes, she needed late nights out at the malecón. But, she also needed a home, and she wanted it with you. She opened the door of her white-walled house; you didn't know you'd never be able to leave. You're always the wanderer, while she sits inside, her hair iron-gray. Even now, years later, she holds you.

The river I fly over
is Río San Juan
always back to the center
of the volcano whose lava
is the everything of us—
always I fly
to Managua, dreaded valley of sun at war,
children who sell candy and piñol,
markets, twisting with flowers,
hardly anything left but plastic colors,
hardly any trees left
in this forest of streets.

She's ridiculously happy. For the first time in her life, she has reached out through the mirror—not Alice through the looking glass, no, she's broken the mirror, dispensed with it altogether; there are so many more important things to look at than herself. She sits on her bed and writes in her journal, telling the story of what her life will be. But at twenty there's a lot she doesn't notice yet, so much she barely sees. The butterflies, for instance, dormant, waiting. Two hanging shadows over her bed. All October, November, they were at peace. Then, she poked them to see if they were still alive, and they fled. For a long time she didn't notice that they were gone. Among the rush of kebab vans and sailing bicycles and high tables and gowns and everything shining, among debates and meditative walks by the river and rowers and college dances and spires that never stopped letting her dream, she didn't see when those butterflies left her—the first out of fear, the second of a broken heart.

The river I fly over
is the Cherwell
to the city built
over one thousand years
of sacred books
I walk through the streets
through the meadows
beneath the glow
of Magdalen Chapel Tower
the gods may be gone, but here
are their halos
and we collect them like litter
from the ground.

This room, this room they made. Everything they put in it, everything they thought would keep them safe. Her uncle's desk and couch covered in flowers, her grandmother's dining room table, the brand-new bed from Sears with a perfectly soft memory foam mattress, old posters now dignified by new Ikea frames. Her friend

Olga's paintings of aliens in lace collars, an orchid they promised they'd never forget to water. This room, this room they made, where so many nights they sat on that flowery couch drinking flowery rose tea, where so many mornings they ate their oatmeal in silence. Only when her tears at last move him to hold her, only in this sorrow does she ever come close to breaking through his distances. Sometimes, when they stare out the window at that high space tower, gleaming red and white, each one sees the opposite color; each one fears they're being led toward separate lives.

The river I fly over
is the Niagara—
a tale of two cities with nothing
in common but proximity,
one the other's shopping mall.
I left one for the other, but always
go back. For me they are
forever attached, two
wings of a cormorant
sitting and waiting
in the naked trees.

"You've changed," David says. "You used to be so special, back when we first met, but then, as the years started going by, every time I saw you, you seemed more normal." "You haven't changed," says Ruth. "Your context has changed, but not your essential 'you-ness.'" But what does it mean, your essential "you-ness"? It bubbles up, it threatens to rip, to unzip the double helix and leave it that way, not to unite each strand with others. I fly through trees that hold up mirrors, birds bearing brooms, I want to go back and down, but there's no place to land that won't make my feet fall off. And so I go, higher and higher into the air, legs sprawled, arms flailing, higher and higher, still with the hope that I can be whole, it's all the same blanket, we really are made of the stars. Maybe we really are in constant flight, and our faith and love are just a sign, a glimmering sign of what's there all the time, maybe we don't ever need to come down.

The river I fly over
is the Lethe
every time I try
to be
who I was.

Your Island

I said I wanted to see another country.
I hoped that, Athene-like, you might show me
the wild Lastrygones, the island of Circe's bliss,
the domain of the Cyclops,
the gentle Lotus eaters in their fields.

Instead, you showed me a treeless island
of linoleum floors and white walls,
a land where no one rushed out to meet me
with steaming pots of soup,
where songs crushed my ears
and I was challenged to games
whose rules I did not know.

I wanted to leave, begged you
to take me to some other place.
with luscious fruits and sparkling beaches.
You shook your head.
I need to stay here, you said.
This is my home now.

I backed away into the dark,
sailed off on a dinghy over the waves,
but every week I came back to see you
standing on your linoleum-covered beach
counting the metallic shells.
I asked, "Are you ready to go?"
You shook your head, defiant. "No."

Soon, companions came to join you
and today I watch you working beside them.
You compile long lists, draw diagrams, eyes absorbed
in the documents before you.
I want to ask you what it all means.

Are there buds in the cracks between the tiles,
hints of jewel in the walls?
Are there emerald-stuffed trees emerging
from the ground, calcite crystals brilliant beneath your feet?

If I explored your island further, would I find
that concrete gives way to forest?
Would I see a chapel not yet torn down,
a place where our minds could touch?

Is there a room you enter without me,
a place where the moon
streams down through a skylight,
where a voice I cannot hear begins to speak?

Madonna of the Two Scars
Our Lady of Częstochowa

The legend says
Saint Luke painted your icon:
Czarna Madonna, Black Virgin Mary
with the Child in your arms.

Hodogetria, pointing the way
to the jeweled boy
as your slim hand indicates him, not you
the source of our salvation.

It's said you reached Jasna Góra—Bright
Mountain—because there the horses
carrying you from one lord to another refused
to go on. You chose Poland as your home.

At so many altars I've knelt before you
and more than your royal robe of fleur-de-lis
more than your jewels, your dark hands, your baby,
it's your scars that command my gaze—

Two sharp slashes down your right cheek.
They say it was a Hussite warrior
bent on abducting you
who made those two scrapes, started

on a third, then dropped dead.
Two hundred years later, they say
your wounded face held off a Swedish invasion
and you were crowned Poland's true queen.

At nine, in the church my great-uncle founded
for your nation's immigrant children
I sang to you and your re-formed country
just three years free of Soviet rule.

I sang and watched the dampening eyes
of Poland's first freely elected leader in fifty years
as he, on his state visit to the US, also kneeled
before your image.

You try to point to your Son
insisting that he, not you, is the Way.
But I can't tear my gaze
from those two sharp slashes

no art restorer could remove.
As a child I was told
to gesture as you do, indicating
others as the sign of salvation.

Lowering my head,
I pointed to all around me,
but couldn't stop wishing
for my own bronze halo.

As my father insisted—
"You have to be more humble,"
I still dreamed of roses
placed at my feet.

As I staved off the Hussite, the Swede,
I still wondered why
after hundreds of years
a woman must be damaged

to be seen.

St. Paul may have stayed at the same hotel where I'm staying
Thasos, Greece

Paul, with his convert's zeal, moving among early Christian communities, Philippi to Thessaloniki, writing letters that became the foundation for billions. Paul, who said if God is for us, who can be against us, who exhorted himself, the good I would do, I do not do, and the evil I would not do, that I do. As a girl I was taught to rein myself in—don't eat too much, don't laugh too loud. A few decades of this and I began to get tired, wishing that Paul might be supplanted by Aphrodite, that she'd appear to me on a beach, but not to make me separate grains or collect the wool of wild rams or descend to the dead—instead, to give me her beauty. *This is the problem*, my friend, a nun, says. *You want all the benefits of mysticism but none of the costs.*

I think of the unpaid debts I've piled up, the lovers I've left, the students whose papers I didn't hand back, the cancer-stricken former teacher I didn't visit before she died. They weigh me down like a purse filled with coins of a currency not in use anymore, make me scared to step into the sea. I have never learned to swim. After seven years of lessons, water remained a careless mother, a disinterested father who would not lift me up. Today I want no more than waist-deep exposure to the sea; any wave is enough to send me running for shore. I picture Paul in his boat, as he rowed from island to peninsula, and wonder if he ever saw the voluminous goddess emerge from the waves on a dolphin's back.

Did he turn away, try to hit her with his oar, rebuke her for her folds of unconcealed beauty? I'm sure she threw back her head and laughed, dragged him into the waves, splashed his face with her foam. Did he manage to swim off, fleeing to the rocks of this peninsula where I now sit, my brow as creased as his? St. Paul might have stayed in this hotel, might have sat in my room writing letters he couldn't know would be read two thousand years later by long-robed men, studied by girls in plaid green uniforms, pored over each morning by me. I'd like to put those letters aside, return to them in the morning. Now that it's night, let me cross the grove of olive trees, climb down moonlit steps, wade into foamy water, gingerly move hands and feet as Aphrodite lifts me—

Nocturne

people I knew, people I held
tried to heal
and needed

are
living on
without me

how to accept
I'm no goddess of love?

deathless
desire
holds the winter
I walk through

while yearning
to stretch and fill, unfold
to expand into a cloak

that would cover all countries
beloved
never walled

I am
one human woman
who sits
in one country

who sweats
four white walls
between

2
Combustion

Assemblage

To desire is to build an assemblage,
constructing a region, really, to assemble.
        —*Gilles Deleuze*

I wanted spell bottles instead of pill bottles.
I wanted bird hotels
instead of suburban little boxes.

I wanted to put out my hands
knowing that you'd come to me,
that you would be the first to call.

I wanted your clocks to stop
your calendar to shred
your wall to make space for my picture.

I wanted to be
perfume sprayed over your back
a rhythm you might dance to

a story
that would not need to die
any sooner than our bodies.

Today
I assemble an archive
of Prosecco and dark chocolate

of massages and polka dances
of hagiographies and flutes and rosaries
of bacon-wrapped dates and waterfalls

of berries and bare feet entwined
of St. Cecilia medals
and medieval maps

with the earth at their center
of kayaks and suns and
green lights.

I assemble a catalogue
that sits on a shelf
nailed to the wall above my bed.

When I move away, I won't
take it with me
nor will I send it to you

and the people
who move in next
will probably throw it away.

Or

It's a word that reminds you you're not the world. You've never liked it. You prefer the ecstatic frenzy of "and," the heaping of spaghetti and chocolate pudding and mango onto plates without any fear of stomachache. But now you're three and a half decades into your journey, and you're in a dark wood, and you think it's Dante's but fear it's Frost's, with two paths diverging, and you can't follow both and be one traveler, and you ask why you have to pick, and you'd like to split yourself in two, maybe a sober daytime Apollonian you and a drunken nighttime Dionysian one, and you try to do this, but there's a limit to how far they'll walk away from each other. You seek a middle way, even though it might send you over the rocks, straight into the brambles. You don't care how much they scrape. A therapist says you need to learn to say "no," that boundaries form identity, but you rally against those who enforce political borders. In 1922, thousands of Greeks were marched into Turkey, Turks into Greece. Today in Thessaloniki, you read a message written on a wall: "Borders kill people." In 1947, India was partitioned. Two million died due to lines drawn on a map. You don't want to be a country with armed guards posted. No, you can't be the world, but even at this age you still want to be the sea, that seemingly infinite network of forkless paths, that blue container of brown and green land. And everyone knows there is only one sea.

Angela Anaïs Juana Antolina Rosa Edelmira Nin y Culmell

No being can contain the blaze that shoots up when a Christmas tree falls on its Candlemas pyre. Anaïs Nin, protean, gorgeous liar, relentless explorer, exploiter, exploited. Psychoanalyst who bedded her patients, bigamist with a one-man-per-coast policy, flame of spirit too much for one body. Anaïs, who left behind pain and love as twin children, who died alone but surrounded, who unveiled so many ways to be a woman, identities not held by her six given names. *You cannot reach unity and integration without patiently experiencing first all of the turns of the labyrinth of falsities and delusions in which man has lost himself.* Her lies were moves in a dance, twists and spins between partners, the tango's dominant stance, the mambo and merengue's sensuous play, the beauty of her bending. How many sets of hands she clasped, how many pairs of eyes, each man knowing he mattered as much as if he were the only one, each woman delighting in shared beauty. *Introspection is a devouring monster. You have to feed it with much material, much experience, many people, many places, many loves, many creations, and then it comes feeding on you.* Lies were expansions to give all she could, reserving some spirit for self and others, a magician pulling endless scarves from her hat, filling huge rooms with carnival streamers, banquets with endless steaming plates.

No

A word like a door with a wall behind it. A staccato that severs and cuts, a word I rarely know how to say, yearning as I do to flow. It's Martian, extraterrestrial, beyond. The "I" is bounded; the "You" stands up like an ocean you don't know how to swim in, a rectangular slab with something to say that you don't want to hear. Hearing it is like lining up to receive food at a soup kitchen when last year you were dishing it out. It's like staring at a stained-glass window that doesn't let the sun straight in. It turns Christ's body back into a disappointing bland wafer. It transforms the Virgin Mary outline in the photograph to a simple hoax. It makes the spell not work, and it means that when you die there may not be any dramatic flash of light. It tells you that you've got nothing left to lose as you sleep alone in a king-sized bed on a sidewalk, a train station floor. It means you might just break into the elements in a table, squares dissolving into circles, circles unfolding into something unseen. It means that pictures of you won't be looked at by anyone even thirty years after you're gone, and if they are, no one will know your name. Sometimes it means a new life you didn't ask for, an old life in shards. It means crumpled paper, a garbage can. The sound of a snap, a tear. A coin falls through a hole in your pocket. There's a smell no deodorant covers. Static on the radio, a paper-jammed printer. A subway mechanical problem. Two options: wait or walk.

Fall, not so dear

You're already present, even though it's June.
I see the aura of red and gold lurking behind the green,
the parched brown of wildfire-scorched land, the chill
of summer rains that contain November's first snow.
I loved a man who adores your months
of big wool sweaters and crackling wood stoves,
church bazaars and applesauce, the smell
of the insides of pumpkins. You know I can't stand
how you steal my light, weigh me down with shade,
make me rise earlier, desperate to see the sun.
How I wish I could go straight from heat to frost,
to skip the slow crumpling of trust, the leaves falling
to form new layers of accumulated pain. I find your red
and orange traces everywhere, seeking the man who
loves your leaves. I want to give him purple
rhododendrons, pink mimosa flowers, and ripe
almonds; lush fig leaves, smooth olive leaves,
and chattering cicadas; watermelons
and tomatoes. I want to give him bonfires
on a rocky beach, a full June moon
casting silver light on Aegean waves
but you won't let me.

if only

you had waited
one more minute
swallowed some pride
put down the phone

if only
you had left the party early
had been wearing the ring
deleted the number right away

if only
you'd had your lucky hat
or rabbit's foot
or at least some bread
to feed the mallards

if only
you'd practiced in advance
taken the time you needed
called him one time less

if only
you'd stopped smoking
gotten up early each morning to write
kept on with the mandolin lessons
signed up for yoga
psychoanalysis
Ignatian prayer

if only
you'd made it to your niece's dance recital
quit the job like you wanted to
and gone backpacking or back to college
after the kid was born

if only
you'd left the bar
one hour earlier
with a handshake and a curt
"good night"

if only
you'd had some self-control, had known
when to stop writing to him
and accepted you're no Anaïs Nin,
spoken the truth with love,
given the right amount
of yourself—

       not too little,
       not too much.

The Collector

"I'm scared," he says, his voice muffled. Forty-eight years old, he looks seventy. His brown eyes meet mine. "I remember you, but it's hard. I'm scared. I'm losing my memory." Four strokes in one year. The doctors don't know why. I tell him he has to stop smoking. He nods. It's hard. "It all goes," he says, and I know it. I collect guys like him. In church I sit next to a plumber who was in a motorcycle accident and nearly died. He spends the whole service crying, calling out, disrupting the prayers. I take his hand during the "Our Father," hug him for the Sign of Peace. "You're a good woman," an usher says. I shake my head. "Looks can be deceiving. I only give to make up for what I take." In truth I adorn my home with broken brains like paintings. Trinkets. I, too, am messed up in the head. My mind is a maze of hallways filled with statues, busts of gods no longer prayed to. Sometimes it dissolves into a network of tiny rivers that run off course, freeze unexpectedly, break dams, overflow. I can't remember why I hurt the one I most loved. How a bottle of wine on a snowy night in a yellow-glowing room in a city I used to love was enough to make me deceive. Why a book of poems sent in the mail made me lie. Why a Beatles song made me hold onto the person I'd lied to long after my choices had let him go. I try to be a do-gooder, anchor myself in those who need, but water flows wherever it wants. Stars crash into other stars, cracked and splintered. Our heads line up together in a hallway of broken gods.

Error

I call out
of two minds
by wanton ones persuaded

seek laurel trees and dream
of lost homes I can't go back to

do I seek the truth or the way?
Why do I throw while holding
sweet-worded Athena
yearning

There's No Rescuing Anyone

An echo wears flowers, seeks lost homes
spoken into silence

that no longer delights your mornings
with night storms
sweet words
I was no hero, no Perseus

You were made to shine your incense
just your gold-singing snow-angels
untamed on solitary mountains
I came to unchain you, Andromeda

I tried

Postcard from Aliki

Distant Mt. Athos won't let the soft-blue sky erase it.
It juts out, rocks and crags reminding me
that none of us will be here for too long.
Stained black rocks of charred Aliki,
parched brown and green. They can't
forget the wildfire that ravaged here
two years ago, burned the goat
path's railing away. Nor can the
turquoise-jeweled sea conceal
the bare rocks with sharp,
black beds of sea-urchin nails
waiting to trap human feet.
Ghost trees stand like dinosaur bones
in a museum, but at least they don't get
gawked at; they're passed over for those
who still pretend to be lush.
I send you a charred landscape, dust-brown
grass punctuated by a stone wall.
I give you the incessant call of sheep's bells,
the chatter of cicadas that won't let you sleep,
the din of bees and flies along the parched riverbed.
I send you the smell of octopus tentacles, of
fish bones carcassing the beach.
I offer you whatever gods still skulk
among the gray-white temple ruins
and abandoned marble quarries, scowling
at the shirtless tourists who snap
incessant photos, who bear no oblations.

It's only a matter of time before
dry lightning returns, before the whole mass
of dirt and rocks and roots
bursts again into flame.

Rainstorm, far from home

For thirty hours it rains.
The sky becomes a vertical river
determined to swallow this island.
The pathways around the hotel
swell, tributaries of the torrent.

In my room I place cups
to catch the drops
that barge in through the ceiling,
try to sleep despite the drumming.
I think of you, eight time zones behind,

at your desk under the skylight,
the only window in your room.
Whorls of your cigarette smoke rise
as my rain falls.
Before the downpour started,

you answered my two-thousand-word letter
with one: Goodbye. Did you smash
the coffee mug I gave you? The one
with the purple cats on it? You promised me
you'd break it if I decided not to come home

to you. For a moment I imagine it's raining
in your room too. You don't close
that window. Each urchin-drop
stings you, as they pinch me with each hit
to my palm. When I wake up, the torrent

has stopped. Clouds hover above the hills
and the air smells like pine needles
and damp clothes. I descend the rocky
goat-path to the sea, curious to see
if the innkeeper's words are true:

the beach collapsed upon itself;
the shoreline was sliced by rain
that washed away its old sharp pebbles
and left a smooth layer of sand in their place.

Aubade

So many days I rose at dawn
to pray and do last-minute grading

I spooned instant coffee into a mug and left you
in my bed, set the alarm so you'd wake by ten.

You said you hated waking up alone
in my room. I never knew why

you couldn't sleep without the television
and lights left on, why you feared

a tiger stalking my suburban street, black-eyed
children who might knock on the door.

Those mornings are gone now, as are so many
of our conflicts over Frasier and Captain Picard.

I wake up still smelling your lavender
deodorant, the bonfire in your hair.

I wake up still hearing the freight train
that made us dart from the tracks.

Zeibekiko of the Olympians and Me

They're all here. On this mountain
Narcissus stares into his pool. Poor Echo chases him.
Dionysus seeks Ariadne; Apollo runs after Daphne.
Zeus the swan pursues Leda.
Psyche struggles to separate the greens.
Orpheus weeps and weeps as the ground
closes beneath him. His last memory
is of Eurydice's slim, white hand waving goodbye.
Demeter embraces Persephone, holds her tightly,
inappropriately, like a lover rather than a mother, knowing
that soon she will have to give her back to the dark.
For now, their filial embrace covers the earth in green,
fills the sylvan space with the smells of holly and pine.
I traveled four thousand miles to meet this dissonant chorus,
and today, as I stare at the Aegean, I hear them singing.
Back home, a man works twelve-hour shifts.
I wade in puddles of a mostly-dried river; he wades
in dishwater suds covering the floor of a chain
restaurant kitchen. At night I know he clasps
a pillow, imagining it's me. I stare at the ceiling, imagine
Hades, Hephaestus, anyone but him. I need different cicadas
to deafen me—the ones back home are not enough.
I need to spend the solstice on an abandoned beach,
to hear the cacophony of restless Olympians
who dance the zeibekiko, each taking a turn
to improvise a new dance within me.
Down on one knee I clap for them,
nine rhythmic beats. Aphrodite shimmies as always,
Hermes does elaborate flips, Hera whirls and kicks.
Still and silent, I kneel and nod at each,
not knowing whose movements I should imitate,
whose gestures I should believe.

Combustion

Last week your house burned down. The cause: faulty wiring or loneliness, a kiss between acetone and cigarettes. Two of your friends ran off burning while you stood in the yard and threw up. When I heard the news, my first response—after relief that you were alive—was selfish hope that you might come back, seek refuge under my roof. You didn't. It's been a week and you haven't called. I pray for you to Saint Florian, patron of fires, that Roman martyr who refused to burn at the stake, who wasn't good at dying. For centuries Austrians have prayed in his name: "Don't let my house burn down. Let someone else's burn instead." We need the problems of others. As a kid I feared nothing more than each blaze I saw on the evening news. I crossed myself until they thought I was crazy, as if that gesture might make me a saint, as if that prayer were the only thing that could keep my house from bursting into flame.

Río Grande Gorge

Two tall dark walls hide a narrow river, a nearly shriveled rock bed. I stand on a bridge with no barrier to jumping and wonder how many have slipped. There's a helpline for those drawn by the shaking, those who hear that dying river's call. I remember rush-hour city mornings, the entire Toronto subway shut down at 9 a.m., "personal injury at the track level." I throw a pebble through the cracks; it accelerates toward the black river, shrinking to the size of Elon Musk's nighttime parade of synthetic stars. There is no splash, no sign the stone landed, as if there were no rock-bottom to the river, as if one could fall forever, Alice in the magic well. On the cliff human debris has landed: a lawn chair, a garden hose, a red octagon: STOP. I step back from the edge. One of these times I might forget to say "no" when it matters most. I look at the low railing's spray-painted messages meant to save: God loves you. You are needed. In a world of Cheerios, be a Fruit Loop.

Outside the Chapel

Loyola University Chicago

I walk beside a lake
so big one might think it's the sea
but no
it's only a lake

I stand outside the chapel
and wish to go in
and light a candle
beside Our Lady of Guadalupe
or her Polish doppelganger,
Our Lady of Częstochowa

and imagine that flames burn their way
into a parallel universe
where nineteen-year-old you
sat in that same chapel, reading Kierkegaard,
Merton, Dorothy Day
never got buried
by the weight of your own mind

you grew up to be an actor
or musician
who met me, fell in love, and started
a homeless shelter
while playing Beatles songs at wineries
and visiting a different country each summer

but in this universe
you're not talking to me

and I go to meetings
where I read lists of clichés:

let go and let God
easy does it
focus on yourself, not the addict
you didn't cause it
can't control it
can't cure it

it would make a better story
if I could go and light that candle
but there's a wedding taking place
go figure

I can love you as much as I want,
but I can't set myself on a pedestal
as the madonna who will heal you
I can pray for you wherever I want
but I can't light the candle
whose flame comes from another place

I'm left with a chapel
I can't get into
a lake that looks like the sea
but isn't

a fantasy left behind
like a discarded church bulletin

a candle I didn't manage to light
and this poem

Winter Solstice

In the Light of Bernadette Mayer

0.

Starting from zero with six skinned knees
in one year. I fall when there isn't even ice.
Attention is the rarest, purest form of generosity,
Simone Weil said. Will this be the year I learn how to give?
Maybe it's time to embrace unknowing
lasciviously, under red satin sheets.

Last week, as B slept, I placed a stuffed animal beside him:
a dog with black floppy ears, blue overalls.
This man has just turned thirty-five and looks
like his six-year-old son, his sixty-eight-year-old father.
We carry past selves inside us like matryoshka dolls
but are only allowed to buy one train ticket.

If that metaphor is too easy, here's an easier
one: bones. They disintegrate, grow brittle.
Thus far I've not broken one, but of course each day
they're unraveling. B, before you came back
into my life, I dreamed of you almost every night.
That you were a transvestite about to move
into a purple house with hippies. That you stocked
shelves in the grocery store and refused to kiss me
when I came near. Meanwhile, you dreamed that you found me
in bed with another man draped over my body like a
macramé shawl, a crocheted web, an enormous bat.
A demon. Maybe because that is sort of what happened,

except the demon was me. Now we offer kisses
by night and insults by day, like when I tell you
that you should pull off Exit 77 from Highway 80
in Illinois for some really good horchata:

"I'll remember that when I'm a truck driver some day.
I'll remember I loved you."

"All trucks will be driverless by then. And won't you
still love me?"

"You'll probably be dead."

"What makes you think you'll outlive me?"

"If the war comes, you won't last long.
You've never even camped.

Or else you'll
get cancer in your fifties."

Cancer. Six months ago, right at the light's
first gesture toward leaving, I was dividing
my bones, offering them as ritual gifts to two
insomniac men. I dreamed that cancer
had spread through me; I couldn't speak from the pain.
I didn't even want treatment, but my mother made me
accept a last-ditch effort toward redemption, my own
personal Siberia. No, I didn't want it, but six months
later here I am, sitting in your apartment with its stacks
of glass beer bottles and no running water, thrilled
like a thirteen-year-old as for the first time in six months
you take my hand . . . until the road calls again.

1.

"What's with all the books?" the immigration official asks
as I beg to be let from Detroit into Windsor. I debate
over whether or not to fess up to my book fetishism.
I thought they'd ask about the five bags of empty
glass bottles, but no—they want to know why I have
two suitcases full of books. I tell them
I'm doing a project for the Library of Congress, preparing
classes for my students, two convenient lies that just so
happen to be true. Maybe I could make my car
a book-mobile, like an ice cream truck
that children might enter and choose books from.
One of those came to my school each week
when I was ten years old. But I'm too selfish
to give books away. They are my blanket fort, my
comfort bunny, a shell I'd rather not have to come out of.
They mean that whatever highway rest stop I land on,
wherever my car might break down is home.

2.

Driving into Toronto, I think of Gwendolyn MacEwan.
A few springs ago, Sonia and Clara and a few other
Toronto poets and I walked through Mt. Pleasant
Cemetery searching for her grave. It took us a while
to find it. But I prefer to think of her as a teenager, insisting
on the fullness of her name, no longer content
with the childish, monosyllabic Gwen. I picture her
as a teenager, hanging out in bars. She read her poetry
to all who would listen, dropped out of school months shy
of graduation to become a writer, published her first book
at eighteen. I think of her marrying a poet nineteen years her senior,

then realizing her need to stand alone, until she met
another, someone to learn Greek and Arabic with, someone
who also loved Euripides, and sadly, someone for whom
to pour drinks. I think of her need for multiple loves
as I turn off Highway 401 to Avenue Road, pass through
gorgeous Lawrence Park, past the Persian restaurant
I went to with my other love seven months ago,
back when the light was still increasing. "I don't want
to be secondary," he insisted, and I knew just what he meant.
And what had I done, unable to accept the word "or,"
seeking to clip a bit of evergreen from every
tree, to seize a rock from every shore, to create a miniature
of the whole earth in my room while dismembering
myself, placing one strand of my hair in a thousand lockets,
to have a thousand pairs of shoes, Imelda Marcos-like, and cast one
at the side of every road. To make the world a monument to me,
Trump-style with his border wall, determined like
so many others to reconfigure space in accordance with
my own musings. I enter Toronto and see the changes,
the big Nordstrom at Yonge and Bloor, and Kensington Market
with its yellow and purple houses and Blue Banana store filled
with Christmas shoppers and the Film Café with its delicious
caramel hot chocolate, and Knife Fork Book, that weird
poetic loft whose name sounds like it should serve food
but it doesn't, it just has exquisite green and yellow fringed
lampshades, and a cardboard horse head, and portraits
of so many gorgeous women, and fringed Persian rugs,
and brightly colored garments hanging on blue, and a velvet
sofa, soft royal red, Christmas berry red, angry red, menstrual
red, where I sit and write these words and wish I could live
in this city for more than just one day.

3.

If you look at my social media posts from the past year, you'll see a young woman—no, just a woman, no longer young, not yet middle-aged—you'll see her reading at AWP in Ybor City, Florida, and you'll see a picture of her reconnecting with a college friend at a Local Food Summit, and another picture of her eating Italian food with her parents, and a video of her polka dancing, and a picture of her students at the end of the semester, and a photo of her holding her friend's newborn, Rowan, and an image of her being part of a low-budget movie, and another picture of her standing beside an ancient basilica on the Greek island of Thasos, and a picture of her drinking wine at the Australian Embassy to the Holy See, and a grand announcement that she almost won the National Translation Award, oh, so close, and a post about her acting in a local church's Black History Month play, and links to songs she likes, and articles she likes, and a meme with a matryoshka doll standing at a train ticket counter with the ticket seller saying "One ticket, really?"

What you won't see:

all the broken dolls inside her,
the babies sawed in half by a false mother
who took seriously Solomon's prescription,
the collection of shattered eggshells,
their interior life turned to powder—
the ones that in sleep exit her body
and insist on walking different roads.

4.

We're allowed to crowd love in
like a significant myth.

I write so much of myths, of books
in which my names do not appear,
of trying to scrawl my letters in as many
men's diaries and calendars and long poems
as I can. Like Pulitzer Prize-winning Vijay
Seshadri, my first college professor,
who mentioned me in his acclaimed
Three Sections, or David, my love of too
many years, whose photograph I hold
before me, a picture of him at nine sitting
in his grandparents' camper, wearing a yellow
shirt and gray shorts that are too big, soaking his feet
in a blue bucket, not knowing that in ten years
as an Oxonian he'll meet me, not knowing
that in twenty years he'll be living alone
in a city across the sea, this city I only visit now,
but imagine is still a place that I live, and when
the border guards ask why my request for
permanent residency was denied, it always comes back
to his name, and I say no, I'm not going
to see him, even though I invariably end up
standing at his door. I kiss him chastely
on the cheek and still wish he'd fill
journals and journals with me, just as I
have done of him. Somehow a father
seems relevant here, my father who does not
keep journals or write letters or use
the internet, who does not tell family stories—
my father who worked long factory nights
just like Robert Hayden describes in "Those
Winter Sundays," stumbling in blue-black

cold, unthanked until years later, while child-me sat
with my mother, also unthanked, in a big brown
house in Buffalo, New York, wondering when
he'd be home. Thirty years later she's looking
for thanks—for Christmas this year she wants
me to write her a poem. I've got three days left,
and all I know is that this one won't be it. She wants
a flattering poem, not the one I published last year
about my rage at her voting for Trump (though my
father did too—why did I let him off the hook?) or else
the one in my first published book, about her sewing buttons
on my eyes, Coraline-style, though my mother has never
known how to sew. What can I tell her that's complimentary
except that when I think of her, cheese pierogi come to mind,
and taco noodle bake casserole, and chicken
with yellow saffron rice, similar to the rice Magdalena,
the young Guatemalan woman I've adopted so she can apply
for legal status, often serves—yellow rice with peas
and chili powder. Maybe I should write about this,
and tell my mother that all her days of waking
me up early, of ironing my shirts, driving me to school
and basketball and dance practice meant something, that
when I was younger I didn't think I'd want to do that
for anyone else, but now I do, and that after my sort-of
daughter Magdalena's first day of school I took her
out for ice cream—just as you always did for me, Mother,
and that even if I found out she didn't care about me
at all, even if she was just using me for a rent-free
roof I'd still love her as you love me. Maybe I could tell
you that I remember you as the one who had huge New
Year's Eve parties and invited everyone you knew,

family or not, friends or acquaintances you just happened
to meet; I remember you as the one who took me to walk
with the environmental group protesting the cutting
of a forest, who invited Brazilian and Chinese and Pakistani
exchange students to stay in my childhood room
after I left home. I also remember you as the one
who helped me to memorize poems for the Polish Saturday
School's Christmas pageant, who drove me to dance
at nursing homes and community centers in my red ribbons
and beaded vests; I recall how we sang together as if
our whole life were an opera, and here is a photo
from just last month, of you and Dad and Magdalena
in her red Guatemalan skirt, and you may fear the foreigner
but not if she comes knocking at your door. This is how
we trust in the light's inevitable return, transforming darkness
and cold into love, this is how we learn to say "or"
as little as possible, to swell and overflow
like any mother, to say "and" as much as we can.

3
I Do

To the Polar Vortex

After Denise Levertov
January 2019

I know your coldness covers ceaseless movement—
beneath your drifts
of restless snow, inside your ice globes
that turn berries into belated
Christmas ornaments.

Ground me, please,
in giving.

I break off a twig
of last year's mistakes
and place it in my pocket.

Please take me to a snow-covered
wood, then teach me to glide
on a frozen lake
the way I never could as a kid
without falling.

Last year I fell six times
on ice and concrete, skinned
my knees bright red. Please give me
the wisdom those scars failed to bring.

Or if that's too much, share the turquoise
mittens B made me, crocheting for three full days
two Christmases ago. I lost them
on the subway. Let them be found
by the one who needs them most.

By your giving, may some grace return
six months from now, pouring water
on summer's dryness. Let me distribute
your gifts and your stories

of a cold light that can't be extinguished
of mercy that thaws and abounds
in melting snow.

Simone Weil answers her letters

Every day they come in crates, these letters from the living.
St. Paul brings them to my room.
Each one bears a question: *Is affliction inevitable?*
Must love mean non-attachment? My favorite:
Why is life not fair? Then, the personal inquiries:

Why did you do it? Why did you have to give so much that you shrank
so thin? You could have lived, kept on writing. You could have reached
past iron curtains, thrown water on the fires of 1968, borne witness to
dissolving empires, surging dreams. I'd like to write back, but letters
aren't sent from heaven.

I reply in smells. The aroma of graphite pencils
in an inner-city Chicago classroom where a young girl studies
parallel lines. The smell of crunched autumn maple
wafting in through an open window, filling her with joy. A sudden
whiff of honey settling over a neighborhood that normally stinks

from the oil refinery. A smell of May magnolias for the white-walled
room where people wait for death. For the weeping mother whose
child has died, a scent of boysenberry syrup from her own childhood,
then a splash of mint from the garden where she conceived her
beloved babe. For the recovering alcoholic,

a smell of melting chocolate. For the prisoner, the smell of buttered
corn and melon from the picnics he can't go to. I know such small
comforts aren't enough, just as eating only my ration
and dying wasn't enough, as eating more and surviving also would
not have been. There is only one Enough, and I can but point to it.

If God exists, why did my husband come back from the war
without a leg? Why is there nothing we cannot lose?
I wish I could tell them that now, as then, I still
don't know the answer—that, when they weep,
angels and saints weep too.

salvation's name was Carmen

my uncle became an architect
moved to California in 1960s
and married Carmen from Mexico City
she changed her last name to his: Mrówka
the Polish word for "ant"
that takes love

she met me just a few times
on their trips to the East Coast
"we have a picture of you on our wall"
she told me, then twelve years old,
greasy-haired and gangly.

what could she possibly see
in a gawky white girl from the suburbs
a girl who looked down
and covered her face with her hands
when she talked
a girl who didn't make eye contact

"learn Spanish," she said
"you can do it"
more than that—
"you need it"

what did she think I was missing?
I wasn't an "at risk youth"
I said no to sex and drugs
my grades were impeccable

but somehow she knew
my own language
wasn't enough
for everything I needed to say

salvation's name was Carmen
with her thick accent, her chiles
rellenos recipe, her evangelical
Christian music

but the only proselytizing she did
was to insist I repeat
those words I struggled
to hear on her tongue—

maybe everyone needs
a redemptive handrail
a lantern, radical light

maybe everyone needs
a Carmen
to tell them they don't yet know
how to speak

I talk with Mary

We sit in her kitchen, sip wine from stoneware mugs, pass photos, compare stories. She speaks of her fear when the angel arrived, when she said "yes" despite her shame. She tells me how, hearing the news, her betrothed shook his head, walked away when she wept...then returned the next day and took her hand. I tell her that not long ago I witnessed a different annunciation, the chance to become a mother by signing my name on a line. She nods as I speak of armed borders, of children crossing deserts alone, of metallic blankets, crowded refugee camps without soap. I tell her that when I met the beautiful seventeen-year-old who needed a guardian to apply for legal status, I saw something in her eyes—a flame, a love. I couldn't just call her a ward. Suddenly I realize. "That was your son," I say. She smiles, her eyes filled with light.

Then I ask her my questions. I ask about her own flight after that terrible birth. "We never thought we'd see home again," she says. I ask about the day her son got lost, about the moment she found him in the temple, standing tall before the elders. "I was furious, but wow, did he stump them," she beams. I tell her that mine has also preached, that she thanks Adam and Eve for the life we've been given, that she recently spoke in a college class called "God is not white."

We talk about our fears: hers, that her son will be killed by the state, mine, that my daughter will be deported. She takes my hands in hers. They are smaller than mine, but firm, brown, covered in tiny spots. We say nothing. We sit like that for a while, silent. The sun begins to descend. Other tasks call each of us—clothes to wash, bread to bake. Her son is out on the road, but her brother is coming back from the city soon, so she's hoping he'll bring news. My own dear girl is expecting me. She makes tamales for supper, listens to Enrique Iglesias while solving quadratic equations. As she plants tomatoes and peppers in her garden, she's waiting for me to come home. I drink one last drop from the cold stone mug. Mary and I agree to meet next week—same time and place. She squeezes my hands, then releases them.

Magdalena

Having risen in the morning on the first day of the week, [Jesus]
appeared first to Mary of Magdala [...] She then went to those who
had been his companions, and who were in mourning and in tears,
and told them. But they did not believe her when they heard her
say that he was alive and that she had seen him.
—Mark 16:9–11

First witness to the Resurrection, you were the one
who set out in darkness, came to the spot,
saw the stone rolled away,

went running to tell the apostles
who didn't believe you

not only because
you were a woman,

but because you didn't have a passport
or even a green card

because you worked in a back kitchen
under a false name

because your English
had a heavy accent

because you still preferred tortillas over bread
and said our hamburgers were the worst food you'd tasted

because you didn't know how to drive, still wishing
for a store and school close enough to walk to

because you'd crossed
behind a "No Trespassing" sign.

Previously, I'd been a faithless apostle.
Like them I fled from the foot of the cross

flitted between distracting lovers and lies
hid for long hours at work

returned each night to a cold, dark box
heat and light turned off

poured myself a beer
to drink alone.

But today when I come home
the stove sings with boiling

carrots, your potato soup
steaming corn tortillas

I sip your *arroz con leche*
while you savor my chocolate chip cookies

you don't ask
if I believe in the Resurrection

you just request
help studying for the citizenship test

and the marvelous story you offer
is that of your own desert crossing

the garlic you stuffed in your pockets
to keep the dogs away

the river's piercing water
the squad car waiting on the other side

your resurrection tale, like hers, is a question
a dare, a rebuke, a demand:

Magdalena, apostle to the apostles
today I give you my answer:
I believe.

History Lessons

My Not-Daughter

I try to become your mother by signing on a line. First, I must cross two languages. Ixil is a coat that surrounds you, protecting you from the white walls' coldness, the waiting rooms and questioning eyes. It guards you from strangers who, though bringing milk and good intentions, don't understand. Nor do I. Your own mother is now a face on a screen, a photo by your bed, someone you hope to see again. Someday. I nurture you in my way, buy you jeans, correct your spelling, drive you to dental appointments. You make me tamales, plant tomatoes and beans on a bare patch of land beside my house. Yes, I will sign. I promise to give you a bed, a roof. I offer to hold onto your hand, though your mother I cannot be.

The Dishwasher

I walk into the restaurant where you work and ask for you: Magdalena. The hostess stares at me blankly. "Magda-who?" "Maybe she's at your other location?" I persist. "No one with that name works here." "She's a dishwasher," I say. Her eyes grow clear. You emerge from the kitchen, apron over your T-shirt and jeans. 10 a.m. on a Tuesday. The hour when you should be studying for a math test, not scraping bits of fake-egg into the garbage, not loading heavy trays into a machine. Not meeting a lawyer who seeks to help people who've crossed imaginary lines remain in their chosen home. It's snowing in April, sleeting ice. The first blooms have frozen. Spring hesitates. Your papers, late. Snow falls. You wash dishes. You've worked for a month, back in the kitchen where customers don't go. None of the servers seem to know you.

How The Other Half Lives

"Translate it for me," you command. It's for your US History class. Shining September; you live with me and go to school. I tell you about tenements crowded with cigar workers, wives and husbands and children up from dawn, working late into the night. I tell you of wealthy landlords who lived in posh neighborhoods and didn't say where they got their money. I tell you of my Polish great-grandparents, their journeys over the sea, how they, like you, came here without money or English, how they, like you, swept floors and worked in factories. "When was this written?" you ask. "1890." A century and three decades compress; I may as well have said "last week." I go on about people twenty packed in a house. "It was horrible then," I say. You look to me and smile. "At least they knew they could stay."

1898

You hand me the paper. This week's lesson: the Spanish-American War. "This was the moment when US imperialism firmly took hold," the textbook states. I show you a map. You label Philippines, Cuba, Puerto Rico. Point to your own country. Seventy years later, it too would feel my ancestors' talons. Could it be that your own journey across borders also began in 1898, with Hearst and Pulitzer, "Remember the Maine," with Rough Riders galloping through Cuba, with betrayed Philippine nationalists shaking their fists? The United States of America, once a freedom-fighter, now a self-crowned king, sets millions running from bombs and pesticides. Its victims come to its door, demanding to be let in. You, one of them, look at me with a question: "Can I really count on you? Are you here for me?" I made a promise; I signed my name, but you know that my life, like my country, is full of bullion and debt, Times Square and vast deserts. Weapons. Once I said I wanted no children; I tried to build a wall. Your brown eyes hold a question. "Will you let me in?"

Saving Private Ryan

Neither of us can believe that Mr. Simmons has made you spend four class periods watching it. You look at me, disturbed, puzzled. Forget D-Day...How to explain World War II when I haven't helped you with your homework on World War I, when you're an 18-year-old with a sixth-grade education who grew up in a village of five hundred, when a big part of you just wants to work day and night and buy some land back in your country. But your lawyers say you need to sit in a classroom and learn these truths. I do too. The Jews—you've never heard of them. "They were the first to believe in one God," I explain. You nod. "In the 1930s, in Europe, a group of people decided they were bad and all needed to be killed." I say the word—*genocide*. Your eyes flash; you lower your head. "Like my country in the 80s," you say. Clarity appears. You know more history than I do.

Graduation

Last week I drove you five hours to immigration court in Omaha and feared I'd be coming back without you. We crossed the land of the Ho-Chunk, the Báxoje, the Ponca. You hail from the land of the Maya. So many transplants to this land, immigrants like me, truly believe that a blonde-haired judge has the right to declare whether or not you can stay. After five minutes he pronounces her decision: denied. One last appeal remains. Your lawyer pledges to keep fighting. You keep silent the whole ride home. But today, you don a lilac dress, new leather shoes; the satin blue gown adorns you. I wish that judge could be here, sitting in the bleachers alongside hundreds of families; I wish she could see the siblings and cousins who have come from other towns to clap and cheer for the first person in their family to graduate from high school. I wish she could see you cross that stage, shake the principal's hand, pose for the picture I take alongside other proud parents. "Magdalena!" I call. Your eyes blaze. You lift them at the sound of your name.

Pray Without Ceasing

Follow the voices from city to city. Speak to the prophets of stairwells, the sages on street corners. Resolve to share a home with others, to flatten the boundaries between servant and served. On the Greek peninsula of Athos monks and hermits pray; since the first century no woman but Mary has been allowed to set foot there. You know this rule was mistaken; you know where the source of life resides. Marry a woman with two children. They will remain yours after the third is born, after the beer bottles pile up, after the tattooed men come and won't leave. They'll remain your children after the divorce. Pray through it all, even when you don't know who hears. Read Dante one canto at a time; draw a cartoon for each one. Sometimes you'll wonder about the lives you might have led, the movie actor you once dreamed of being, the musician you were for a while. You're thirty-five with debt piled up from your two years of college, thirty-five with anxiety and a scruffy beard. You wash dishes at two bad restaurants. Sometimes, you ask yourself why. A brief break comes when one of the guys in the back offers you a smoke, or when your lover pulls up to the window at Wendy's to order a small order of fries, or when she meets you in the lobby of Olive Garden and gives you a hug, and the young servers giggle. Pray as she leaves you in the lobby, as the water seeps into your boots, as you sing to the radio (once a singer in an acid folk band, you're no longer too proud to sing top 40). You do not need a hermitage. You always say you're going to take a week to camp alone in the woods, but you never get around to it. You'd miss Ambrose's mischievous smiles, Audrina's drawings of smiling flowers, Armond, with his finger twiddles, now that he claims he's too old for hugs. No, you don't need to travel to the mountain of Athos. Each day it comes to you.

This is not a homeless shelter

After Jamaal May
For Hope House, Dubuque, Iowa, 2018

Did you think there wouldn't be books here?

Did you imagine white walls, strict rules and regulations, curfews, a line of sad people waiting for others to dish out soup for them?

If you pictured concrete slabs, fluorescent lights, large rooms filled with bunk beds—here, that's not what you'll find.

This is a place where people sit at long tables, where dishes are passed family style, carrots, pork, greens. It's a home where the faces of Gandhi and Martin Luther King stare out from walls, where posters assert that money is not speech.

This is a place where in November we honor the dead, where in December we discuss the origins of the Santa Claus story, where we celebrate the Easter Vigil reading Thich Nhat Hanh, where all year long old men sing "Take me home country roads" on Sunday nights, where children draw rainbows on the ceiling.

This is a place where an architect designs a villa in California, where a twenty-two-year-old edits his first feature-length film and enlists sixty people to produce it, where we sit to memorize new alphabets.

This is a place where a small boy whose father was deported learns to read in two languages, where a man who suffers from alcoholism befriends a squirrel named Scruffy, feeds him peanuts out of his hand.

This is a place with floors of dark wood, with shelves and more shelves of books, poetry and history and chemistry, where there's always someone sitting down to read them.

This is a place where people ask just why they need to get a job, why jobs are needed at all, why should we aspire to own a home, why can't we just share.

This is a place where giving and receiving are one, where I belong and so do you, even though you think you don't, even though you live across town and take pride in giving a few dollars a year to those poor homeless you've not yet managed to visit, those poor disadvantaged who probably don't even read books.

A Gift from Hephaestus

On Leaving Greece

I watched Thasos shrink in the distance as the ferry moved farther away. Soon, it was another layer of lush hills blended with the landscape. I didn't want to sleep on the bus, didn't want to miss the chance to watch green holly bushes and olive groves recede. But still I dozed. Later, at a rest stop, heavy with the smell of powdered sugar, sweet *loukomi*—I wanted to carry that smell, along with the sharp, clear aroma of ouzo, the prickly green holly, pink mimosa flowers. But I couldn't keep them.

Now, the smell is of seaweed as I lie on a beach outside Thessaloniki. Mt. Olympus peers out at me from under rain. Does one of the deities notice me searching? Maybe Hephaestus, the carpenter and blacksmith god, maker of Achilles' shield, trapper of his adulterous wife in chains. I can almost see him, looking my way and scowling. He knows I'm going back to piles of unpaid bills, ungraded student essays, two lovers I still can't choose between, anxious parents who wonder why I've not called. To-do lists kept

for years with unrealized ambitions: write the novel, learn Arabic, read St. Teresa's *Interior Castle*, Hofstadter's *Godel, Escher, Bach.* Clouds caress the tip of Olympus. The waves wash my feet. Sea, hills, sky, various shades of blue. Maybe Hephaestus is calmer now. Maybe he's not making me a chain or a chair I won't rise from. He smells of petroleum and water. Could he be making me an airplane? Surely he knows how to do that now, build a vessel I can use to return to this place where I am no one's daughter or teacher or beloved, where velvet sands embrace me, where my body can touch its salty primal home. But no. When he descends the mountain, stands on the beach before me, the gift he offers is small: a metal box with a stone from Olympus. "Add a stone from every beach you walk on, every mountain you climb. As you fill it the box will expand; there will always be enough room. Place in it the most shining amethysts, calcite, marble, quartz, maybe even a diamond someday. It will get heavier; the weight may make

your shoulders slump. But with each stone your strength will increase. In every room where you rest, take these gems and set them before you; I promise to make them gleam. There will be many beaches, many hills, many rooms. Some day, when the box's weight becomes too much, come back to Olympus and return it to me. Many fires will have ravished this landscape by then, but tough saplings will sprout in burnt wood's place; you will return to find these hills green. May the journey be long; may the day be far off. I wish you a lifetime of the most brilliant jewels."

Uruguayan poets live forever

On the gray days
in the dark nights
I like to think about 90-year-old Selva Casal
sitting in her wheelchair and writing poems about justice
or making abstract sketches
while her 92-year-old husband Arturo does her makeup.
"She paints pictures and I paint her!" he quips.

On those mornings
when it's hard to get out of bed
I like to think about Circe Maia, another nonagenarian
singing as she works in her garden.
If you make the trip up from Montevideo to Tacuarembó
she'll offer you tea, homemade bizcochos,
quince preserves—dulce de membrillo—
show you her nasturtiums, her lavender,
her violets.

At one poetry event at the Decorative Arts Museum
a car pulled right up to the door,
and we thought it was for 98-year-old Ida Vitale.
Instead, a middle-aged man emerged
and like a sprite
Ida came bouncing past us all
from somewhere else.

Not for these women a death by binge drinking—
not for them a head stuck in the oven
or a late-night wade into a lake, pockets filled with stones.

Not for them any membership in the 27 Club
shared by Janis, Jimi, and their own Delmira Agustini—
"la nena," murdered by her husband in 1914.

Delmira, who sought to hold God's head in her hands
who imagined Leda's Swan covered in blood
who exhorted her sister souls—"Never look back!"
They didn't.

Circe, Selva, and Ida
insist on living
as they cook, paint, drink tea
defend convicts, denounce dictators, go into exile
lose children, lose loves, but keep their lives
for as long as they can.

Sonnet

Back and forth on a terrible swing. I'm scared
of stopping. I'm scared of flying too high and jumping
off. An Icarus dilemma, or a Rapunzel one? I'm trapped
in a room. Someone said that if I could just step outside,
I'd finally see the whole house. Hope is the last thing
left in the box. If I give it up, what do I gain?
No guarantees. You gave me my first kiss. It was yours too.
You lifted me on your shoulders for a dance. We both laughed
when you dropped me. Many nights you held me...until you decided
you wanted the bed to yourself. Today, years later, you tap my
shoulder in a half-crowded room. I'm surrounded by old friends,
ghosts of those I knew. I turn. You look at me. "Didn't you think I'd
be here?" you ask. Water into steam, carbon into land. We've both
changed our shape. This is what lets us meet again.

I do

when the archbishop placed his hands
on my sixteen-year-old head
when he anointed me with oil
sealed me with the Holy Spirit
I did not know
he was carving
a space in my head
that swelled into a house
with a roof but no walls
a door that couldn't be shut.

throughout your life
he intoned
people will enter and leave
this house,
this *chuppah*,
this refuge.

some will stomp
through the rooms
with harsh boots.
others will decorate floors
with silk and satin and wool.
you must shelter them all
though none will stay.

since that day
I've not worn a ring.
I've not walked down an aisle

in a white dress.
I've neither donned a nun's habit.
nor borne a child.

instead, I walk
with this space inside me
this open door
these messy rooms

populated by my great uncle's bayonet
from World War I
and the keffiyeh
my grandmother bought
outside Bethlehem in 1974

and the flashing silver flames
Natalie tore from her wrist and tossed to me
when I said
"I like your bracelet"

and the four high school yearbooks
holding photos
of Ashley Dickinson, aspiring biologist,
who once danced to the Beastie Boys
at school talent shows
today, gunned down at thirty-four.

and people come in—
the young superhero fanatic
in the grip of seizures
after the one he loved
married someone else

the heroin addict who believes
the earth is flat
and won't stop blathering on
about the Illuminati

the con artist
who fakes cancer
so that I will give him money

my mother
who calls at midnight
unable to wait in her own house alone
while my father plays blackjack
at the casino.

each day
as I carry these rooms
the only Beloved
never to leave me—
you, the stillness after every long weeping
you, the green flash after sunset
you, the mountain revealed at dusk—

you ask if I promise
to still be a home—
each day
I respond
I do.

Ask for Living Water

"If only you knew what God is offering and who it is that is saying to you, 'Give me something to drink,' you would have been the one to ask, and he would have given you living water." —John 4:10

Imagine that, one late July afternoon, while driving down Highway 20 outside Galena, Illinois, you stop at the scenic overlook rather than passing it by.

Suppose you admire the pastures, rolling hills, small patches of forest; you inhale the smells of thousands of plants that are as nameless to you as to those who first met them.

Maybe you'll lock your red Saab's doors, fumble in high-heeled sandals down the path, gaze up to cumulus clouds against a blue backdrop, take note of birds with black bodies, yellow wings.

At the bottom of the slope a stagnant pond waits. Green algae cover half of it; a turtle suns itself on a log. You don't know why it's calling you, but suppose you listen, entranced, until

startled from your reverie by the arrival of a man. Suppose he starts to talk to you, says he's thirsty, asks for a sip from your water bottle, and you instinctively back away, but something in

his eyes says wait, don't worry, I'm different. You already saw him at the top of the hill, easel before him, painting the scene. Now he stands beside you, plaid t-shirt covered in watercolors,

and he tells you he knows you've been through five bad breakups, that you've cheated and deceived, that you claim to like your freedom but still aren't happy. Suppose right then he says it:

"Come, follow me, I'll give you living water," and all of a sudden you know the names of each plant, each blade of grass, each cloud that forms and breaks. Astonished, you thank him and ask

if he'll be back there tomorrow, and he says yes, and you promise to bring others to meet him. Imagine that you step back to your car, now knowing that it is possible to make each act a

prayer: the cleaning of drains, the paying of bills, the making of phone calls and amends. You are confident that even in the midst of dark November you will find in yourself this place

where ferns touch briers, where this artist shows you his face. Imagine how you'll feel, come January, when you recall that beneath the most solid ice, living water still flows.

The river that cuts a country in two

1.

I met a man who walked beside it every sunrise
taking pictures of lacy ice in December, red-winged
blackbirds in May, flaming leaves in October.
Those dark waves kept his cracked soul
from breaking.

2.

In the mornings I hear trains
rumble and call to me from its banks.

3.

"Does it still have fish?" a Canadian friend asked.
Though it has borne hundreds of years
of barges and pollution, the morning fishermen know
it does. Bald eagles have returned. Turtles
and otters line its tributaries. Life prevails.

4.

Some days the closest I come to faith
is knowing the river will outlast me.

5.

The first time I visited this town, I exclaimed,
"I've never seen the Mississippi River before!"
"Do you want to dip your toe in?" my future colleague asked,
our laughter drawing spirals of white condensation
in the December air.

6.

When I moved here, I insisted on living
A ten-minute walk from the blue.

7.

One month after we met, we walked beside it on a warm
August night, talking about books. When we saw the green
light on the bridge, we both exclaimed, "The Great Gatsby!"
We looked at each other, laughing, taking each other's hands, certain
we'd be lifelong friends.

8.

I've lost her now
but I still have the river.

9.

There's a plan to build a pipeline under
its waves, to pump tar sands oil from prairies
into lakes. Original dwellers struggle to stop this.
Many join them, crying necessity. It's okay to ignore
a "no trespassing" sign when the house is burning.

10.

"Water is life"—
That's not just a slogan.

11.

It took me some time to accept
that I'd chosen these bluffs and caves
just as they'd chosen me. This flyover country,
this drive-across land, the bluffs of this winding
ribbon are home.

12.

The river that cuts a country in two
also binds it together.

A Small Thing

And in this he showed me a little thing, the quantity of a hazelnut,
lying in the palm of my hand, as it seemed. And it was as round as any
ball. I looked upon it with the eye of my understanding, and thought,
'What may this be?' And it was answered generally thus, 'It is all that
is made.'
—*Julian of Norwich*

A small thing, small as a hazelnut, small
as the wild black raspberry
ripening on a woodland bush,

small as the hummingbird's
heart, beating much too fast for life—
I want to go home a voice inside cries,

but no home exists, the world cracks
in two, no paternal hand reaches
for mine.

A small thing, small
as an acorn, a cottonwood seed, small
as a green bloom of moss, an inchworm

hanging from the sky,
held in the pierced hand of a God
some blame.

for bringing this plague,
but I imagine just as confounded
as we.

A small thing we seek
when after months without hugs
my feet reach for yours:

we stop our walk
to lie outstretched, our faces more
than six feet apart

while the soles of our feet embrace
and the clouds float above.
two choices: four walls or one sky—

and the human world we knew
transforms faster than our feet can follow.
With nowhere to run, there remains

a small thing, small as a hazelnut
an apple seed, small as
a child's laugh, an ant's leg,
a pen's tip, a bee's wing,

small as a virus:
life's first built block
held in the pierced hand

of God

Breath

New Mexico Museum of Art, May 2021

For my first visit to a museum in seventeen months, I don a mask, take a wary breath, and enter a narrow corridor filled with photographs of "For Sale" signs dividing the desert. I cross a courtyard lined with frescoes, to an exhibition on breath: paintings of strange sine curves meant to represent our inhalations. Before me a bubble expands on a screen, then breaks into an image of a man in a choke hold. "I can't breathe," the mantra of 2020, the suffocation of racism gnarled with the breathlessness of pandemic. Will this long year of plague recede into the background like a distant blue mesa as I turn around and drive home across the plains? Doubtful. It will remain like the white rocks of Plaza Blanca, a twisting reminder of finitude. We are each King Ozymandias building electronic self-monuments soon to be strings of nonsense numbers fallen out of use. Daredevil Wim Hoff believes we don't breathe nearly as well as we used to. He wants us to live, to love in the cold. We tend to believe that everything will work itself out somehow—until the day it doesn't. In the meantime, we climb up, we slide down, we work, we walk. We breathe.

Hold On

Ghost Ranch, Abiquiu, New Mexico

I walk on red sand punctured with resilient green. The matrimonial trail, they call it. I stare at mesas and hills that Georgia O'Keeffe painted. The only ring I wear is my high school ring. Twenty years after receiving it, I've chosen freedom over love. Or not. You can love as many people as you want, one lover told me, as much as you want...just as long as you don't succumb to the belief that they are the source of your being. Better to believe in the sun, in red mesas, a cactus plant. Take their light; imbibe their sparse water. Grow from the side of a rock like a spindly tree. Jesus was wrong about the seeds that fell and landed on hard ground. Some of them heard the word that let them insist on growing. Their crooked trunks, their bent branches: a singular kind of preaching. Even now they hear the words. Look how they hold on.

When Scheherazade Fails

I don't win every time.
Sometimes
my cliffhanger endings
don't leave him suspended
as he finds his footing,
climbs out of the trap,
his compulsion to cut
greater than my efforts to save.
His need for repetition
leads him to betray me at sunup
and I lie there, my neck bleeding,
my head a dirty soccer ball
kicked onto the garbage heap.
But at night I stand, pick it up,
reattach it, and, invisible now,
run back to the palace walls.

Passing through them, I listen
as he speaks words of love to another.
As she dresses for dinner
I whisper, urging her to let me in.
I don her shawl, take her place
at the table. I tell him of witches
in the woods, of monks giving blessings
on airplanes; I speak of drug addicts who've
seen the beatific vision, of contortionists
writing computer programs, of an empire
collapsing over a world too small
to hold it, of plants that seek to stop

growing, of a sky that somehow stays blue
while the ill-fated bride sneaks home
and he falls asleep at my side
and as long as there's someone to speak
it's never the end of the story.

Buen Camino

After Elena Ferrante, Those Who Leave and Those Who Stay

As I walk, you walk with me—
twenty, fifty, more than I can count.

You form a procession of angels climbing the mountain, your
footsteps so loud they drown out the song of the white-breasted
desert lark, your all-too-human sweat competing with sagebrush
fragrance.

I called you here, you who no longer send me Christmas cards or
birthday greetings, whose phone numbers I forget, whose addresses
I've erased.

First-grade drawing companion Nicole Maciejewski, fellow pilgrim
around the Cheektowaga cul-de-sac, selling thin mints and peanut
butter patties

each Girl Scout cookie season—here you are now, offering me
a hand to hold for the slippery ascent.

Pablo, of a midnight walk along the Río de la Plata one silver hot
December night, our shoes filled with sand from the beach of a city
that loves the sea—here you are now, showing me which rocks are
safe.

Cecilia, of a dank August stroll along the Mississippi, marching
toward Gatsby's green light—here you are now, warning that the
path narrows ahead.

Ben, of a confused romp down Frenchman Street, both of us strangers in the city of jazz and colored beads, the drunk leading the drunk past the tap dancer with a baby in his arms—

here you are now, tapping my shoulder and pointing up
to the soaring hawk I missed while counting steps.

You, my brothers, my sisters, my loves—it is not your death I grieve but my own, since I am the ghost who seeks to haunt the paths you have chosen without me.

Maybe not even a very orderly mind can endure the discovery of not being loved. And yet still I love—anyone, anywhere, as much as I want—which is why I've called you here

as I approach the labyrinth's center, as I ascend sharp rocks to smooth sands above.

And you have come, shadows whose footsteps I follow
as I dream of a mesa where we might rest together

to marvel at the same red and blue mountains. And if I open my eyes and find myself alone,

I will still call out *Buen Camino*, I will keep shouting love
to each one of you,

even if you won't hear me.

In Praise of Revithia

Thasos, Greece

Revithia, your Greek name so melodious
it could belong to a goddess, so much more
luminous than your supermarket English equivalent:
chickpea soup.

I wait for you as hunters anticipate
a deer, as divers delve beneath the waves
in search for their eight-footed prize.

All morning the wood stove's fragrance
hearkens your arrival, tiny round amber jewels
adorned with silver onions, set with carrot and
rosemary, emerging after hours of refinement.

"I always had the idea
that vegetarians don't actually like food,"
a friend once declared. Clearly he has not met you,
glorious Revithia, with your perfume
of exploded sugar, melting oil, pine.

You are made by a woman who sold diamonds,
by a man who fought battles until both
traded fatigues and transatlantic flights for a home
under a canopy of olives and grapes, for figs and a wood stove.

You are the tiny circles formed
when people come to understand that every "yes"
requires a "no," that poignant refusals trace the shape
of a gem shining with a brightness concealed
while it lay buried in rock.

When I get home I will try to remake you.
Done are my days of cans and quick fixes,
of "just add water"—your sweetness
demands much waiting.

I will soak the dry spheres all night, chop
the onions, add the sugar, the carrots and rosemary—
only at the end comes salt.

And while you won't be the same, still you'll remind me
of marble quarries and blue Aegean waves,
of temples and mountains, of the simple truth
that every "no" contains a jewel,
a sweet and savory "yes."

ACKNOWLEDGMENTS

"Wings of Desire," "June 24," and "Panic" appeared in *Luna Luna Magazine*.

"What Rafa Writes" and "Simone Answers Her Letters" appeared in *U.S. Catholic*. The latter also appeared in *Attention*.

"Or" appeared in *Eastern Iowa Review*.

"Rainstorm, far from home" appeared in *Convivium*.

"Zeibekiko of the Olympians and Me" appeared in *Ocotillo Review*.

"This is not a homeless shelter" appeared in *About Place Journal*.

"I Do" and "Letters" appeared in *Dappled Things*.

"Ask for Living Water" tied for third place in the 2020 New York Encounter Poetry Contest and was published on the festival website.

"Mycophobia," "Nephophobia," "Assemblage," "Angela Anaïs Juana Antolina Rosa Edelmira Nin y Culmell," and "Sonnet" appeared in *Beltway Poetry Quarterly*.

"Magdalena" appeared in *Pensive Journal*.

"A Small Thing" appeared in *The Buffalo News*.

"salvation's name was Carmen" was published in *A Lantern, Radical Light*, an anthology published by the Women in Translation Collective based at University of Wisconsin-Madison.

"The River that cuts a country in two," "During the Sixth Extinction," and "History Lessons" appeared in *Vita Poetica*.

"In Praise of Revithia" appeared in *Anglican Theological Review*.

"Buen Camino" appeared in *Braided Way*.

"Madonna of the Two Scars," "Outside the Chapel," "To the Polar Vortex," "Uruguayan Poets Live Forever" and "A Gift from Hephaestus" appeared in *Live Encounters*.

I thank Scott Cairns, Laura Reece Hogan, and Jon Sweeney for selecting my work as second-place winner for the 2021 Paraclete Poetry Contest. I thank Robert Edmonson, Lillian Miao, Jessica Schnepp, Jenny Lynch, Danielle Bushnell, Rachel McKendree, Olivia Tingley, and everyone at Paraclete Press for editing and publishing this book.

I thank the following organizations that have supported me on my journey: The Algonquin Square Table, Writing Workshops in Greece, the Collegeville Institute, New York Encounter, *Presence: A Journal of Catholic Poetry*, University of Dubuque, the Catholic Worker Movement, Dubuque for Refugee Children, and St. Vincent College.

I cannot name all of the many teachers, mentors, editors, family members, and friends who supported me in bringing this book to fruition, but I want to mention Jonathan Allan, Lauren K. Alleyne, Leonora Arieh, Eric and Brenna Cussen Anglada, Susan Antebi, Ramiro Armas, Terry Barker, Jonathan Barz, Lauren Beard, Sean Benson, Mirdza Berzins, Robert Biniszkiewicz, Ronna Bloom, Allan Briesmaster, Grace Cavalieri, Laura Cesarco Eglin, Jacinto Ceto Corío, Brenda Clews, Carolyn Clink, David Clink, Fr. Wulfstan Clough, Patrick Connors, Daniel Cowper, Simone Crookston, Magdalena Cuyuch Corío, Elizabeth Deifell, Kristin Dykstra, Dale Easley, Giles Edkins, Jo and Keith Edkins, Stephanie Ells, Parson John Emery, Esther Fine, Suzanne Fitzgerald, Kate Marshall Flaherty, Michelle Gil-Montero, Meg Goehrig, Leslie Gold, Susanna Cantu Gregory, Rebecka Himmelsbach, Rebecca Howard, Luciano Iacobelli, Tina James, Tom Johnson, Andrew Jones, Paula Karger, Jesse Lee Kercheval, Dan Lawson, D.S. Leiter, Sara Lindey, Dennis McDaniel, S. Keyron McDermott, Scott and Kathryn Mackmin, Michele McKinlay, Frederick Miller, Mary Ann Miller, Rhonda Miska, Matt Muilenburg, Aimee Nezhukumatathil, Hoa Nguyen, Irena Nikolova, Carol and Nicholas Pitas, Robert D. Pohl, Joseph Allen Ray, Kalissa Reeder, Néstor Rodríguez, Megan Ruiz, Mary Rykov, Emmalea Russo, Pouneh Saeedi, Marta Ester Santiago Pérez, Mallory Saylor, Jessica Schreyer, Jayme Schmitt, Vijay Seshadri, Justin Shapiro, Wacek and Mute Sobaszek, Ricardo Sternberg, Judith and Terry Schmidt Stewart, R.R.S. Stewart, Dane Swan, Tamara Trojanowska, Father Anne Tropeano, Ruth Vincent-Schechtman, Kevin Wilson, Sara Williams, Nicole Willson, Eric Emin Suleiman Wood, Suzie Wright and so many more. Thank you.

ABOUT IRON PEN

O that my words were written down!
O that they were inscribed in a book!
O that with an iron pen and with lead
they were engraved on a rock forever!
—Job 19:23–24

Outcast and utterly alone, Job pours out his anguish to his Maker. From the depths of his pain, he reveals a trust in God's goodness that is stronger than his despair, giving humanity some of the most beautiful and poetic verses of all time. Paraclete's Iron Pen imprint is inspired by this spirit of unvarnished honesty and tenacious hope.

ABOUT PARACLETE PRESS

Paraclete Press is the publishing arm of the Cape Cod Benedictine community, the Community of Jesus. Presenting a full expression of Christian belief and practice, we reflect the ecumenical charism of the Community and its dedication to sacred music, the fine arts, and the written word.

SCAN
TO
READ
MORE

www.paracletepress.com

You may also be interested in . . .

There is a Future

A Year of Daily Midrash

poems by

Amy Bornman

www.paracletepress.com